PAINFUL

—— to ——

Painless

JANETTA WALKER

WRITERS REPUBLIC L.L.C.
515 Summit Ave. Unit R1
Union City, NJ 07087, USA

Website: *www.writersrepublic.com*
Hotline: *1-877-656-6838*
Email: *info@writersrepublic.com*

Ordering Information:
Quantity sales. Special discounts are available on quantity purchases by corporations, associations, and others. For details, contact the publisher at the address above.

Library of Congress Control Number: 2021908719
ISBN-13:   978-1-63728-362-2   [Paperback Edition]
                  978-1-63728-363-9   [Digital Edition]

Rev. date: 04/28/2021

CONTENTS

To anyone struggling in a relationship. Take the time to realize that when you apply so much focus on who was not there, you take away a lot of energy and focus from the ones that have been there! I pray this book encourages you to find the strength to move on and shift your focus on people and relationships that give you the same beautiful energy you give out and just pray for the ones that do not!

ACKNOWLEDGEMENTS

Just wanted to take the time to say thank you to my amazing husband for always pushing, encouraging, and motivating me. Thanks for believing in me when I did not believe in myself!

Thanks to my beautiful children.

Lexy, my oldest baby. Trae, my only son. Zi, my youngest baby. I am extremely proud of you all, and I am so blessed to be your mom.

To my sister Janae and my best friend Shannon thanks for always cheering me on. I appreciate you both so much.

Shannon, you have always told me since day one I was great with words. Look, now I wrote my first book!

Thank you to all my family and friends that has been in my corner and supported me throughout my life. Your prayers, love, and support I do not take lightly. I hope you enjoy the book.

CHAPTER 1

I Got Questions

In a deep sleep during the week, I suddenly woke up angry again. I've been angry for many years now. It's like every time I try to release it or let it go, it comes back and in full force with so many questions running through my head: Where is my father? Why do I have to continue to live this life without my biological daddy? He claims to love me, but his actions don't line up with his words. What did I do to deserve a parent like this? One who couldn't care less to love me like I wanted to be loved; one who couldn't care less to hug and give me the affection I needed when I felt stressed out, kiss me on my cheek to give me the security a woman needed, and assure me that no matter what I went through, Daddy would be there. I had none of this, and I was angry about it. Tears started to run down my face as I felt the pain from being disconnected from my father began to take over my body. I could not think straight and quickly seem to get very hot from the feelings of rage, anger, and bitterness. This feeling took over anything good I had going on, took away my happiness instantly, and depression moments soon followed.

CHAPTER 2

More Questions

I sat in the bed that day wondering why I kept finding myself here so upset. Was it because he continues to come in and out of my life? Was it because the lifestyle he has chosen year after year, day after day, minute after minute seemed way more important than me? Or did I just feel too good to have a parent like this? Will I ever have the relationship I longed to have? The way everything was going in my life, I felt it would never happen. I got up that morning and did my regular duties. As I continued on with my day, the rage came down, and I started to feel my inner side become peaceful again.

CHAPTER 3

Realization

Most days, I could stand up tall, love others, and enjoy my day; but some days were not like that. When you have something that you want to happen so bad and it continues to linger with a slight of hope, it can—and will—take all the energy out of you. Some days, I had no energy to be Janetta Walker. I must say when it comes to that point, you need to get help and discuss these issues with someone. I didn't get help for a very long time. I never really talked about it with anyone but my husband, and I wish I would have done something more at that time. I spent too much of my life worried sick of someone that did not want the connection I wanted with them, and for what. Recognize what you spend most of your energy on. Once this is done, decide quickly if it's worth it. Does the energy you're putting in bring anything to the table such as positive vibes, happiness, joy, peace, love? If not, instantly find ways to let go of it. Life is too precious to waste time. Time waits on no one. Don't continue to waste your precious time on things that bring nothing to you. From a young child all the way up to my twenties, I was focused mainly on asking, where is my daddy? I had several things in mind to focus on, but I was not focused like I should have been. Life became frustrating. The frustration came from why I could not move past this issue and why anger kept showing up in my life. How could I find myself in these rage moments again and again?

I'm grown with an amazing husband and two children at the time, why must I continue to ask where Daddy was.

CHAPTER 4

The Conversation

I got married at the age of twenty. I could not believe God sent me such a wonderful man in a moment like this where I was hurting and couldn't love the way I needed to. In my mind, I thought I was ready for this. Maybe this connection would take away the previous pain and hurt I experienced. Maybe the brokenness would end. Maybe I could feel the security and affection I longed for. In my heart, I just couldn't get there. I prayed daily for strength and to take this disconnection phase out of my life. Some days were so good for me, and some days were so bad. My dad was released from jail, and I thought I would bring it to his attention how I felt. I cried my heart out, "Why can't you just do right? Am I important to you or not?" As my dad started to speak, I could see his body language change. His eyes got big, and his breathing got heavy; everything seemed to get intense, and I noticed the rage moments I experienced so often were coming out of my dad. That moment got serious. The spirit of heaviness and darkness took over. I didn't know how to feel. I sat quietly and listened carefully. He stated to me, "Daughter, you know my mom died when I was a baby. I don't know my father. He gave us up soon as my mom died. He put us in foster care when we were very young. We were in foster care until our aunt came and got us."

My aunt was such a sweet woman, and she tried so hard to raise my dad and his brother to the best of her ability. But my dad started running the streets at a very young age and instantly involved himself with the wrong people. He seemed to be amazed about this lifestyle because he would constantly run to the streets with no hesitation. I quickly sat up in my seat and cleared my voice, and then with all the power in me, I stated, "Dad I understand your mom passed and you didn't have a relationship with your father." I prepared myself to say the next sentence. I could feel myself getting mad; my heart was beating fast, my eyes felt like they were turning red. The rage moments I've always tried to escape were coming full force.

I then swallowed my spit and aggressively said, "How dare you not get your life right so your kids wouldn't have to endure the same pain, disconnection, and uneasy feeling that you experienced? How dare you be this old and still use the circumstances of your childhood as an excuse?" Breathing hard with tears running down my face, I calmly said, "I am done with this conversation there is no point in talking to a loser." A shocking feeling came over me, and in my mind, I was thinking, did I really just call my father a loser? I quickly went in a daze because I couldn't believe that word came out of my mouth. As I glanced in the air with disbelief, my dad said, "Excuse me, don't you ever in your life call me that again regardless of how you feel about me and what I've done or didn't do. I am Daddy, and you will respect me. The feeling of rage was coming quicker than it has ever came before. I wanted to ball my fist up and, with all my might, punch him into his next life to see his maker. But instead, I got up and walked out. Walking quickly to my car and speeding off, the words repeated in my head, "I am Daddy...you will respect me," and again, "I am Daddy...you will respect me." I put on my gospel music and started to pray.

CHAPTER 5

Prayer

Prayer

Father, in the name of Jesus, Lord, I thank you for this day. I thank you for your goodness. I thank you for waking me up this morning and starting me on my way. You're an amazing God, and I thank you for everything you have done. I ask that you give me peace over this situation with my father. I ask that you touch his mind, body, and soul. Help him to understand that no matter what he's been through, he's still able to get things right. He still has time to do better and be better. He can get the help he needs. He can leave the drugs alone. He can go back to school and learn a trade. Help him realize that he is beautifully and wonderfully made, that he can do all things through Christ that strengthens him. God, help me to be sensitive at the times I need to be when dealing with him. God, I'm crying for help. Help me with my mouth to make sure I say things that are nice and encouraging. That I can say things that may somehow, someway make him change or even think about changing. I praise you in advance for the victory over this situation. I thank you for giving me the strength I need to make it through. Days I feel useless, down, and discouraged, it's always something that comes my way to uplift my spirits, and I thank you for that, God. Thank you, Lord, for everything. Amen! Amen! Amen!

CHAPTER 6

Reality

After praying this prayer, peace came over me, and I continued on with my day. I started looking for things online to help me deal with anger issues, depression—things to help me deal with a parent not wanting to be involved with a child. I found several articles on various topics and began reviewing some of them. I needed help. I needed to accept my dad for who he was. I needed love and a hug.

As I continued to look through articles, I kept coming across a specific sentence over and over again. It's a sentence we've all heard before, but sometimes, it's hard for us to grasp it and move on from the fact that "we can't make anyone change."

If people don't want to change and be a part of your life, we have to learn how to move on from that. Pray and move forward. This was difficult for me—to accept who my dad was. It was hard to accept he didn't want to be involved like I wanted him to be, and it was more difficult to accept that I didn't seem important enough for him to change and do right.

Sometimes in life, we focus way too much on the people that aren't doing us right, who don't call, who don't show us the love we want and end up overlooking the great people placed in our lives to love us, comfort us, and be exactly what we need and want them to be.

I wrote this book for that specific reason: to hopefully encourage someone to not dwell on the pain and disappointment of the absence of others for too long. When you dwell on things too long, you can easily miss out on a good thing God has for you. Not only that, but the good things you have suffer from receiving the love they deserve from you.

CHAPTER 7

Think about It

Thinking about your life and all the things you have been through, how many people have you tried to change or wish were different? We must realize we can't change anyone. We must give the people we love to God and allow him to handle it. God is the person that makes all things new as long as the person is willing and ready. At this moment, I'm praying for anyone struggling in relationships. I'm praying that you, sir or ma'am, will no longer seek validation from your parents or anyone else, that you will pray for your parents and no longer be mad or be bitter about anything they did or didn't do. I pray that you can move forward in positive and happy thoughts. That any negative thoughts or thinking would quickly be removed and be replaced with God's good word. There are times we want God to give us grace and mercy, but we can't give any to the people we're surrounded by.

In July of 2017, I cried out to God and asked him to forgive me for being so harsh and hateful towards my dad and to give me the patience I needed to deal with him. Trust me, I cried out several times before and prayed daily, but there was something different about this night. I did not get up from the altar until I knew my mindset was changed and that I was totally set free. I lay and cried for over an hour. There were a few ladies that lay and prayed with me. It felt so good to finally cry out to God for help, not in a bitter, mad way but a sincere cry for help. That night, my life was changed forever. The next week, my dad called from prison, and I told him I forgave him for everything and that I would be praying for him. Praying for his mind, spirit, soul, thoughts, and I let him know just because he made a few bad decisions, he still could get his life on track. I also asked my dad to forgive me for my behavior and harsh words in the past, and he was happy to do so.

The funny thing is, I was supposed to be a Christian; but for a long time, forgiveness was not in my heart, and I could say things to my dad that was nowhere near godly. Christians need to check themselves daily because most times, we're the most judgmental hateful folks out there and will gossip in a minute. If you claim Christianity, I ask that you take a closer look at your life and see if you have lived close to the Christian life the Bible lays out for us.

Strive daily to live a life of genuine love for yourself and others. Forgive and move forward past things that you're not profiting from.

CHAPTER 8

Our New Journey

After forgiving my dad in 2017, we began a new journey. A journey of love, understanding, and forgiveness. He went to prison again, but this time, it was different. I would take his calls with no hesitation. We would discuss various things such as family issues and how I felt about him over the years. I would spend time daily praying for him. I often spoke life to him, telling him he still had time to get it right with his other kids and start building a relationship. He told me that is what he wants, and he has been putting as much effort as he can. I am so proud of him.

I tell my dad how strong and smart he is. My dad is such an intelligent man. He had a desire to go to the NBA but did not have the right people in his corner to help get him there. My dad has been in the streets for many years. His mother died when he was a baby, and that was when his father decided he did want to care for him and gave him up to another family member. He has felt rejection, neglect, and disappointment all his life.

I felt bad for him that he never got to experience the model family life and love from his parents. He has had to figure out a lot of things on his own and had to grow up quick.

When you do not experience love and do not have the guidance you need in life, it can be very hard to maneuver through life on the right track. What I noticed is a lot of people experience so much trauma and never seek help, get help, or try to manage the pain and release it. So many are holding on to hurt and have not let it go. That pain and that hurt is eating them up inside every single day. If my dad had reached out for help, he could have been in a better place then and now. Therapist, mentors, life coaches, good family examples are out there to assist if you want the help. While my dad is in jail now, we are trying to be the best guidance and example for him. My husband talks to him often and we speak positive things and we pray. My dad is reading books, praying, and talking about starting his own business when he gets out. Not only that, he is communicating with his sons and putting effort in trying to build a relationship with them.

People in jail are very intelligent people. We must stop being so quick to give up on them. When my dad went to jail the prior times, I would barely take his calls, and I would not write him back when he wrote letters. Well, there goes that rejection feeling he has always felt facing him again. I realized I did not want to reject him anymore, and that was why I prayed to God to give me strength to be a better person to him. Now that we are building a relationship, I can hear in his voice that he has something to live for. I can tell he is happy and ready to stop giving his life to the prison system. He knows he has purpose and is ready to start living the life God has for him.

I look forward to my dad's calls every day. Each call, he would say, "Please know your dad loves you and do not ever feel like I do not. I loved you from the day you were born and always had strong feelings about being a dad." One thing about my dad is he has never denied any of his children, and he would always take the time to check in with all of us. It did not matter if he were on the streets, in jail, in situations he had no business being in; he would always make a quick call and say he loved us and he was okay. And for that, I was thankful.

We have been on this new journey for almost three years, and I can honestly say we are in a better place, and it feels good. It feels good to get my feelings out and him to get his out too. I like our daily phone calls, just checking in to see how each other's day has been. We have been communicating very well and taking all feelings in consideration. Not only that, he talks to his grandkids and gives good guidance on how to remain focused in school, told them to practice hard and give it their all in everything they want to do. Lastly, he would tell them how much he loved them. He would say, "You know Papa loves you, right?" My kids enjoy his calls and appreciate him checking in. My husband and dad talk often as well. They discuss how to make our families stronger, business concepts, and they also discuss strategies that they want in place to make sure when he gets out this time, he will start on the right track and stay on it. They read books and then discussed them from men's point of view and how they could strive to be better men every day. I adore their relationship and thank God for it.

One day, my dad called and thanked my husband for taking so good care of his daughter and grandkids. He said, "My daughter is so blessed to have such a good man like you." I cried so hard that day because that was so sweet of my dad to recognize and praise him. My husband had to deal with me and my daddy issues for so long, and I thank God he never gave up on me or my dad. Such a blessing!

CHAPTER 9

Wrapping Things Up

To wrap things up, I pray this would be an encouragement for someone to forgive, reevaluate the life you proclaim, let things go, move forward, and to not allow anyone or any circumstance to define who you are. It is okay to get life coaches, mentors, and therapists involved. You are not alone in whatever you may be facing. Please take note there are still good, genuine people in the world that would not mind helping you just like they helped me. Allowing pride to run your life can be a bad thing at times and can allow you to miss out on blessings and connections. Try to be open-minded as much as possible and show love even when it is hard to do so. Sometimes, we settle in things when God has a bigger and better plan for our life.

Trust God through all processes and let him do the work for you.

God bless!

ABOUT THE AUTHOR

Janetta Walker was born in Omaha, Nebraska. She is married to the love of her life, and they have three beautiful children. She loves to read, listen to music, and uplift others daily. She is a positive person that spreads so much love, positive energy, and kind words daily! A few people call her sunshine because her presence and personality light up a room!

She loves God, her family, and to see others working in their full potential and purpose! She hopes to inspire many people across the world to never give up on life no matter how hard it may get. She has pushed through many struggles of her own and so much emotional pain that she wanted to share a piece of it through this book!

9 781637 283622